DATE			

ALSO BY ROGER RICCO AND FRANK MARESCA

With Julia Weissman
American Primitive: Discoveries in Folk Sculpture

ALSO BY FRANK MARESCA

With Robert Gottlieb
A Certain Style: The Art of the Plastic Handbag, 1949–59

BILL TRAYLOR

BILL TRAYLOR

HIS ART—HIS LIFE

Frank Maresca / Roger Ricco

ALFRED A. KNOPF   NEW YORK   1991

This Is a Borzoi Book
Published by Alfred A. Knopf, Inc.

Copyright © 1991 by
Frank Maresca & Roger Ricco

All rights reserved under International and Pan-
American Copyright Conventions. Published in
the United States by Alfred A. Knopf, Inc.,
New York, and simultaneously in Canada by
Random House of Canada Limited, Toronto.
Distributed by Random House, Inc., New York.

Library of Congress Cataloging-in-Publication
Data

Maresca, Frank.
    Bill Traylor: his art, his life/Frank Maresca,
Roger Ricco.—
1st ed.
        p.   cm.
    Includes bibliographical references.
    ISBN 0-394-58702-2
    1. Traylor, Bill, 1854-1947.   2. Afro-
American painters—Alabama—
Biography.   3. Primitivism in art—
Alabama.   I. Ricco, Roger.   II. Title.
ND237.T617M37   1991
759.1—dc20
[B]   91-52859
                    CIP

Manufactured in the United States of America
First Edition

FOR ANTOINETTE
A GOLD STAR

SPOTTED DOG

Poster paint and pencil on cardboard

$6^{1}/_{2}'' \times 10^{1}/_{4}''$

CONTENTS

ACKNOWLEDGMENTS

Acknowledgments and thanks no matter how hard you try always seem to sound like you have just been presented with an Oscar. But it is true that a book, like a film, is always a team effort. And we would like to thank the following people who helped to make this book possible:

Charles and Eugenia Shannon
Marcia Weber
Luise Ross
Donald McKinney
Carl Hammer
Gina Chiaro
Lyle Rexor

Linda Safran
Allison Rowell
Elizabeth Holderried

Anne Orlando
Priscilla Baker
Mrs. Horice Perry
Miriam Fowler
Blanche Balzer Angell
Oren Slor
Antoinette White
Lanford Wilson
Scott Photographic Service

and our friend and editor
Vicky Wilson

**CONSTRUCTION WITH
FLEEING FIGURE**
Compressed charcoal and
poster paint on cardboard
$13^1/_2'' \times 7^1/_4''$

PREFACE

Our initial exposure to Bill Traylor came in 1981 when we heard that a colleague had located a number of drawings that were tremendously exciting. The story was that they had been done by an ex-slave some forty years ago. The work had been produced during a three-year period, by an eighty-five-year-old man who worked on a downtown sidewalk in a small Alabama town.

As dealers and collectors, we were filled with curiosity and optimism about this chance to acquire the work of a new self-taught artist. We visited the seller's apartment. A table was piled with perhaps one hundred and fifty drawings. From the moment we began to leaf through them, we were stunned. Here was something different, great, and truly unexpected. The images were absolutely fresh and at the same time they were almost familiar, like a face you can't quite place. But we hesitated and became practical. Who would understand and appreciate this work? What would the costs of marketing be? Hesitating to make a decision, we left the apartment and shortly thereafter the seller consummated a deal with someone else.

In January 1982, a haunting drawing of a coiled snake on a stained cardboard was featured on the cover of the catalogue of the landmark show *Black Folk Art in America, 1930–1980* at the Corcoran Gallery of Art in Washington, D.C. This show traveled across the United States creating shock waves of excitement.

Bill Traylor was discovered. And now, forty-odd years after his death, his work is being celebrated.

Frank Maresca
Roger Ricco

BILL TRAYLOR

Monroe Street,
Montgomery, Alabama, 1939

REMEMBERING BILL TRAYLOR:

AN INTERVIEW WITH CHARLES SHANNON

From 1939 until Bill Traylor's death in 1947, the artist Charles Shannon was his friend and supporter. Shannon is responsible for the encouragement, collection, and preservation of Bill Traylor's remarkable body of work. He is also the primary source of information on the artist's life history, circumstances, and artistic practices. The following interview with Charles Shannon was conducted by the authors in Montgomery, Alabama, in November 1989.

Q. You were in Montgomery and knew Traylor from the time he began to draw, through his productive years, until his death. Tell us a bit about yourself when you met Traylor.

A. In 1939 I was twenty-four, living and painting, with the help of a Julius Rosenwald Fellowship, in my cabin studio about forty miles out in the country from Montgomery. I came into town on weekends to see my family and friends and to teach a night class at New South, a cultural center a group of friends and I were trying to get started. Saturday mornings I would go down on Monroe Street with my sketch pad. This was black territory—a rich and interesting world unto itself where, on Saturdays, the country people would come in and park their mule-drawn wagons down the middle of the street while they went about buying provisions and mingling with friends along the sidewalks.

Q. And it was here that you first saw Bill Traylor?

A. Yes. One such morning in the spring of 1939 an old black man was sitting on a box on the Monroe Street sidewalk. He had a white beard and was bent over. It looked like he might be drawing. When I got close to him I could see that he had a little straight-edge stick and was ruling lines with the stub of a pencil on a small piece of cardboard.

He didn't look up. I watched him a minute and moved on. I couldn't get him out of my mind. The next morning I went back to see if he was still there. He was, sitting in the same place by a board fence behind which was a blacksmith's shop. He was drawing and I went up quietly to stand beside him. His cardboard was about five or six inches square. Drawn in pencil silhouette, images of rats, cups, and shoes were arranged neatly in rows across the space. I talked with him a bit and learned that he was living in the back room of Ross Clayton Funeral Parlor a block down Monroe Street. Later, I was to see how he rolled out some rags on the floor among the caskets to sleep.

Q. This was the beginning of a process that was to continue for a long time.

A. It was. He worked steadily in the

days that followed and it rapidly became evident that something remarkable was happening: his subjects became more complex, his shapes stronger, and the inner rhythm of his work began to assert itself.

Q. All of the earliest pieces are done in pencil; when did he begin to use paint?

A. I can't remember exactly, but within two weeks after he started drawing I began to bring him supplies—pencils, better cardboard, the full range of poster paints and brushes. Later, other people brought him crayons and compressed charcoal pencils, with which he produced some beautiful drawings, and some pastels which he never touched.

Q. In the photographs of Traylor he sits by a building and a Coca-Cola box. Did he move from the location by the fence where you described seeing him first?

A. In the summer of 1939, not long after he began to draw, he moved across the street to sleep in a little shoe-repair shop on North Lawrence Street. Again, Bill slept on his palette on the floor and when the shop opened in the morning he got out on the sidewalk where he set up in an unused doorway. This was the back end of a pool room. Here he was out of the way, behind a Coca-Cola box that was part of an old Jewish man's fruit stand. A shed roof extended out across the sidewalk over the fruit stand and Traylor . . . providing him with shelter and also light by which he could work at night. Just around the corner on Monroe Street was the Red Bell Café and pool room. Bill ate there and used the bathroom there. His friends from the country would come in on Saturdays and park their jugs of kerosene and sacks of feed and seed in a circle around him for

him to guard while they went off to have a few beers. His work flourished here. It was here that he produced practically all of his best pieces.

Q. Did he work every day, and for how long?

A. All day, every day. There may have been a few days when he didn't feel well that he would not have worked so much, but there were very few times, when I went by, that he wasn't drawing. And I don't think I ever went down there that I didn't find him. On summer evenings he would be sitting there at nine or ten o'clock smoking his pipe and drawing.

Q. How long a period did Traylor work?

A. Three years, from the spring of 1939 to the summer of 1942, when he left Montgomery during the war. He told me he did no drawing during the war and the little work he did after his return was not good and I didn't save it.

Q. Tell us more about his physical appearance.

A. He was a big man. He had farmed all his life and had big, capable hands that swallowed up the little pencil he drew with. You seldom saw him standing, but sitting you were aware of the solid forms of his upper body and bald head. He sat quietly.

A kind of beautiful simplicity came through, a selflessness—something impersonal. I hardly knew him before I painted an eight-foot fresco of him. That's how he affected me.

Q. You say he farmed most of his life. We know he was born a slave on the Traylor plantation. What can you tell us of his early life?

A. A few years ago we sought out a member of the George Traylor family, who still lives on the plantation, to learn what we could about Bill and the early days there. Mrs. Rosa Traylor did not remember Bill, who had left the place some fifty years previously, but she knew where he must have lived—in a little house that once stood down by a creek. She was, however, very knowledgeable about the territory and provided us with information about her family's history.

Bill Traylor was born a slave on the George Hartwell Traylor plantation on April 1, 1854* near Benton, Alabama, twelve miles from Selma and forty miles from Montgomery. George Traylor bought the plantation in 1833 and it consisted of 388 acres. On April 2, 1865, in the final days of the Civil War, Wilson's Raiders attacked Selma and demolished the armament factories there, then turned toward Montgomery. Some of the stragglers

*Lowndes County census of 1900 lists a Bill Traylor as having been born on April 1, 1856.

came by the George Traylor place. They walked through his house and took the meat from the smokehouse and rolled it in the dirt. They burned his cotton gin and one hundred bales of cotton.

Q. Bill was eleven years old when the war ended and he remained on the plantation?

A. He did. When Bill was twenty-seven, George Traylor died and his son Marion, then nineteen, became the owner of the plantation. The 1888 field notes of Marion Traylor show that a survey was made of the place and listed on the survey team was "Bill Traylor, colored, flag man." Bill was fifty when Marion died and his widow, Annie Boyd Traylor, continued to live on the plantation until her death in 1934, the year Bill turned eighty. A few years later, he came to Montgomery.

Q. Did Bill talk to you about his life on the plantation?

6

BLUE MAN ARCHING
Poster paint on cardboard
$11^3/_4'' \times 8''$

HORSE AND RIDER
Poster paint on cardboard
15″ × 13¹/₂″

A. A little, from time to time. He said that he raised twenty-odd children. He told me how he would go down into the woods in the wintertime and bring wagonloads of leaf mold out to plow into his fields to build up the soil. We were in the Depression years and he felt that most farmers raised too much for cash and not enough to eat. He said, "You could have that building over there full of money, but you couldn't eat it." Explaining why he finally left the plantation, he told me, "My white folks had died and my children scattered," so he came into town.

Q. You have written that when he first came into Montgomery he worked briefly in a shoe factory, but had to quit because of his rheumatism. If he could not work, how did he support himself?

A. A federal welfare program, known as "relief," provided him with help.

I think he got about fifteen dollars a month. But then, a nickel would buy a hamburger and a dime would get you a "plate lunch." Mr. Ross, the owner of the funeral parlor, let Bill sleep in the back room of his shop. He, like other black businessmen, was asked to take in homeless people during the Depression.

Q. After he began to draw, was any significant amount of money derived from the sale of his work or was that really just loose change?

A. Just loose change. If anyone came along and wanted a drawing, he could have it for whatever he chose to give. Bill was amused, he said, "Sometimes they buys 'em when they don't even need 'em."

Once, as a result of the article in *Colliers* about him, a Chicago man bought a Traylor mule from me. I charged him twenty-five dollars for it and took the money to Traylor. He said, "Just keep it for me." I said,

"Fine, you know where it is if you need it." He never did ask for it, but when he died his daughter called and asked me for it and I sent it to her.

Q. Did Traylor have relatives in Montgomery that he was close to, that took care of him?

A. The only relative I knew of before World War II was a daughter who lived in Detroit. There was a time, about 1940, when he went to Detroit on a bus. We helped scrape up some money to help him buy a ticket and thought we would never see him again. In a couple of weeks, though, he was back. He was very upset that the bus lines did not provide restrooms for black people. It turned out, after the war, that he had a daughter in Montgomery and I presume she was here before the war, but he never mentioned her then. I don't believe he saw her then either.

Q. Did he ever express a desire to

UNTITLED
Pencil on cardboard
22″ × 14″

Monroe Street, 1939

return to his old home place in Benton?

A. No, but one time I did suggest that he might enjoy riding out there and looking around. He never got to go anywhere and I thought he might enjoy the change of scenery. He was not all that enthusiastic about it, but he went.

Q. You drove him out there?

A. Yes. He didn't lead me to the old plantation, but into the village which lies along the banks of the Alabama River. As we drove slowly along the sandy lanes, he saw an old black lady bent over working in her garden. "Pull up over here," he said. I eased up close to the lady and she came to the car. He leaned out the window to embrace her lightly and they murmured gentle greetings to each other. I moved to my side to give them their privacy and they talked along in soft, low tones. I had no idea what they were saying or who the lady was. In a few minutes they grew silent. Bill turned to me and said, "Let's go on back now." I said, "Okay." And that was our trip to Benton.

Q. About his work, his materials and his methods—what prompted you to bring him the poster paints?

A. He was working only with a pencil on cardboard and he was outlining shapes and filling them in with tone. I felt that if it were me, I'd prefer to use paint and brush. Showcard color was simple and easy to use. He took to it and became masterly in various ways of painting with it.

Q. He seemed to prefer cardboard just found on the street, boxes, display cards, and the like. I don't see much in the way of formal board that he used.

A. You're right. I brought him poster board, but he preferred his cut-up boxes and the backs of the window cards. He would stick the nice clean boards I brought him over in the corner with his boxes and after a while they would be sort of ripened off where he would use them.

Q. Why do you think he preferred the more imperfect boards?

A. He liked his dirty boxes, I think, because the smudges, cracks, stains, and the irregular shapes of his boards generated visual activity that he responded to. It was obvious in some cases. For example: he found a counter display card with staples in it where men's handkerchiefs had been attached—Bill drew a pigeon picking at a staple. Another window display card had a thin slot in it and Bill drew a figure peeking into the slot. In "Brown House with Figures and Birds" (page 76), the way the figures are pulled tumbling back into the bulge at left and the birds are swept up the right curling edge of the board back into the center of the picture, one feels had to be in response to the shape of the given space. In the "Blacksmith Shop" (page 13), the upward movement that begins with the angular cut into the bottom of the board is picked up by the legless man's rocker and the curving tong, and swings up into the spinning figures at the anvil. The action of the mule is in response to that movement. The gray patch where the paper is torn from the cardboard is so perfectly integrated into the design that it is not perceived as a flaw.

Q. Tell us what you remember of the method in which Traylor worked.

A. Very often, though not always, he started out using the little straight-edge stick he had the first day I saw him. He always held that in his left hand with his knife as he drew. A horse began as a rectangle for the body first. Then he drew long thin triangles for legs, wedgelike shapes for the neck and the head, all ruled with his stick. Then, still with pencil, he would fill out the forms freehand with curved lines. Sometimes he would lay in tones with pencil which he would leave in or paint over.

Q. He was very direct, wasn't he?

A. Practically no erasures. In that one over there with the house in it, he erased the entire house because he didn't like the way it worked in the composition. That was an exception where he did erase. Normally, he put it down and that was it. He dipped his brush in the jar of paint and then applied the paint to the drawing, not going to another surface to mix his color. I never saw him mix one color with another. Sometimes he thinned with water to get washes and utilize transparent-opaque interplays.

Q. How large did Traylor work?

A. His largest pieces were probably 30 to 36 inches and there were very few of those. Working on a drawing board in his lap, it was more comfortable for him to work on smaller sizes. So, by far, most of his drawings were done on pieces of cardboard that fit easily on his 18 × 24-inch drawing board.

Q. We know that Traylor attached strings to his drawings and hung them on a fence nearby, thus exhibiting his work. Was this something that someone suggested to him?

A. I don't know. I always assumed it was his idea to tie the strings in them and hang them up. But somebody else could have suggested it.

Q. In a photograph of Traylor we see young black boys around him. Was this a common occurrence and were there other people who were around Traylor regularly?

A. The boys were street kids who came

BLACKSMITH SHOP
Pencil on cardboard
13³/₈″ × 26¹/₄″

occasionally to sit with Traylor and watch him draw. They were never a bother to him. A few feet away was the shoe-repair man who gave Bill a place to sleep. The Jewish man and his wife who had the fruit stand were sweet people and were very kind to Bill Traylor. Black men who were out of work drifted around the Monroe Street area and at times some of them would be seen sitting on the box next to Bill. One of these men became a frequent companion and taught Bill how to write his name; you can see Bill's signatures develop on his drawings from illegible ones to quite readable ones. Bill was in and out of the restaurant and pool hall every day and had friendly relations with the proprietors of those establishments. On Saturday people from the country, whom we've already mentioned, were regular visitors to Bill.

Q. Tell us about some of the people in the neighborhood who became his subjects.

A. We were just looking at a drawing of the blacksmith's shop that has in it the little legless man. He has the rocker stool and the devices that he used in his hands to propel himself along—that was one. His name was Jimmie, and Traylor would probably see him every day.

Q. You saw him also?

A. I saw him often. In fact, I had him come and pose for my art class. Then, there were the men that had one leg, there were two or three of them around the area where Bill sat. One has a peg-leg, by the way, and the others have crutches. None of them are of Bill Traylor himself because he made the drawings before he lost his leg.

Q. He drew male figures carrying a satchel of some kind. What was the significance of that?

A. They represented suitcases. Where Traylor sat was across the street from what was called a "hotel," it was actually just a few rooms upstairs for black people. Also, he was on the route from the hotel to the train depot and the bus station, just a few blocks away. So black people often passed by him going to the hotel. That is where he saw the people with suitcases and the Mexican people that he drew who were transient job seekers.

Q. He depicted white people as well as blacks?

A. He did sometimes. Their faces were left just in outline, without tone. That was one way he depicted white people. And he showed me another way. He placed his little stick down on the profile of one of his figures and said, "Now you see there, when the stick touches the nose and the chin but it doesn't touch the lips, it's a white man." He said, "If it touches all three, it's a black man."

Q. Did Bill Traylor know that you were an artist?

A. I really don't know. I don't remember telling him that I was.

Q. Did Traylor ever deal with religious subjects or talk to you about religion?

A. He never talked about religion. He did draw two crucifixions, one in tempera and one in compressed charcoal. And he did three "congregations" using a circle with figures around the outside representing the congregation, and in the circle a central figure with arms outstretched was the preacher. In an early composition, he did a tree full of birds and possums that he called a "Possum Hunt" (page 174). Dogs were barking up the tree, one man had a gun, a woman waved a bottle, and the figure kicking up his heels and twirling his hat on his finger, Bill said, was the drunken preacher.

Q. I notice that a number of his figures are pointing their fingers. Is there any explanation for these?

A. About one of them he said, "This man is making a speech." Some of them are street preachers. He used the pointing finger in different ways. In an "Exciting Event" (pages 86, 152, 154), it meant "There he goes" or "Watch out for the snake" or something of that sort. Sometimes it seemed to mean "I say unto you."

Q. We know that Traylor was given his first show at New South. Tell us a bit about New South.

A. Early in 1939, a group of friends and I got together to try to start something that would alleviate the barrenness of our cultural landscape. We managed to generate some activities that lasted about a year. Whatever anyone wanted to try, we would. We got a meeting place and called it New South. It was a third-floor space in a downtown building consisting of several rooms originally used for cotton sampling. Many skylights and windows down one side made for a beautiful light. The walls were predominantly a light blue but the scaling paint revealed many other colors. We held exhibitions of pottery and paintings by Southern artists. A discussion group chose to study a hefty report on economic conditions in the South and met weekly to discuss it. We sold a few books. The music group had record concerts of classical music with lectures and discussion. A Viennese refugee held a class in German. I had a class in painting and one in life drawing. A writers' group produced a brown paper magazine featuring poetry and short stories. Everybody participated in putting on Irwin Shaw's *Bury the Dead*. It was here that we hung Bill Traylor's first show

DOG AND PIG, VERTICAL
Poster paint and pencil on cardboard
22″ × 14″

DRINKING BOUT WITH KEG
Pencil on cardboard
21³/₄″ × 13³/₄″

New South,
Montgomery, Alabama, 1940

less than a year after he had begun to draw.

Q. Was the show received with interest?

A. Well, mostly among the people already participating in some New South activity or other. Several of them pitched in to help hang the show, maybe a hundred pieces, and to help produce the catalogue. On the cardboard cover of the catalogue we used a silkscreen reproduction of Bill's drawing the "Sea Cow." The inside pages of brown wrapping paper contained a short essay and linoleum blockprints of two more Traylor drawings.

Q. What was the name of the cover drawing again?

A. "Sea Cow." Bill Traylor said, "I don't know what dat is, I calls it ma 'Sea Cow.'" In the essay we were pretty rhapsodic about our "people's artist." We say, "Because his roots lie deeply within the great African tradition and not within that of the White man and because beautiful and living works have resulted, Bill Traylor is perhaps one of the most significant graphic artists the Negro race has yet produced in this country."

Q. You mentioned once that he came to see the show.

A. Yes. I went and got him, managed to get him in the car, which was no easy task, and to New South. It was on the third floor and the ceilings were very high, the steps very long. It must have taken us a half an hour to get him up there. One step at a time, we finally worked our way to the top. He went in and, steadying himself with his two canes, he looked around with no change of expression, he just looked. He leaned over and, pointing with his cane, said, "Lookit dat man 'bout to hit dat chicken." He went around and looked at every picture. After one time around, when he got to the end, he was ready to go. So we took him back down the stairs, back to where we got him on the sidewalk, and he sat down on his box, picked up his pencil, and started drawing. There had been no acknowledgment that this was his work, and he never mentioned his show again. Nobody was less impressed with Bill Traylor than he was himself. It didn't bother him that people didn't swarm around his exhibition, and very few did, by the way.

Q. Did the newspapers write it up at all?

A. I think some member of the writers' group at New South wrote the PR and took it to the newspaper, but that was it.

Q. Did anybody buy anything?

A. Nobody bought anything. The works were not offered for sale, but anyone wanting Traylor drawings would be directed to him.

Q. I take it that not many people

availed themselves of that opportunity.

A. A few people may have bought a few pieces from him. After the interest that the show created had died down, practically no one paid any further attention to him.

Q. But you continued to see him regularly?

A. I persisted because he enhanced my life so much. I couldn't wait to see what he would do next. In 1941 I went to West Georgia College as an artist-in-resident, but I returned to Montgomery on weekends and would always see Bill. His work piled up behind the Coca-Cola box and I would take it and store it to preserve it. I would see that he had what he needed to keep him going, and he came to think of himself as working for me.

Q. When and how did his productive time end?

A. Pearl Harbor was in December 1941.

I was drafted in June 1942. Bill Traylor left town shortly after that to live with his children in different Northern cities.

Q. But he did return after the war?

A. Yes. A few weeks after I returned from the Army in January 1946, I found him sitting in his old place by the fruit stand. He looked bad and had lost a leg to gangrene.

Q. Do you know what caused that condition?

A. He just said he had gangrene. He said, "I begged them not to cut it off. I told them I wanted to go out like I come in." Shortly afterwards, however, the agency that supplied his welfare check discovered that he had a daughter in Montgomery and insisted that she take him in off of the street.

Q. Did you continue to see him at his daughter's house?

A. Just once, when he sent me a note to come to see him there. I found him

sitting under a fig tree in the backyard. He had his drawing materials beside him, but nothing much was happening. He was miserable and he asked me to write a letter to his daughter in Detroit to ask her to take him in. I wrote the letter for him and the daughter replied that she loved him very much but it would be better if he stayed where he was.

Q. Do you have her letter? Could we hear what it says?

A. Yes. It is written in pencil on red-lined tablet paper. It says:

". . . I'm very inconvenienced to keep him here with me because I'm in a 2nd floor apt. and have no help or way to get him back and forth up and down the stairs. If I would take him with me he would stay only a week or two and worry about going back to Ala. He has been here 4 times already [presumably during the war, 1942–45] and worries about

**FIGURES/CONSTRUCTION,
YAWPING WOMAN**
Poster paint and pencil on cardboard
13″ × 14″

one place like he does the other one and I think he's in the best place in his condition. He's lived with each one of his children in Chicago, New York, Philadelphia, Washington, and other different places but won't stay with either. We all love him and want to keep him but he just won't stay so he's in the best place. . . . I want to thank you very much for having such interest in my Father however I think he's in the best place and I would be so grateful if you would try to explain things to him."

It wasn't long after we got this letter that I received the one from Bill Traylor asking me to come to see him in the hospital.

Q. Do you think Traylor considered you to be his best friend?

A. Yes, I do. He must have felt the esteem in which I held him.

Q. He wrote to you from the hospital?

A. He was in a nursing home called the Fraternal Hospital. It was torn down many years ago.

Q. Can I ask you, do you remember what was said to you in his letter?

A. I have it here.

Q. Who is it from?

A. It is from Bill Traylor, but it was written by someone else because he couldn't write. This helps to establish the date of his death, which came just a matter of days after this letter. It's dated February 3, 1947. It says: "Mr. Charlie Shannon, Number 2 Lucine Street," which is incorrect, "Montgomery, Alabama. Dear Sir, I am asking you to come to the Fraternal Hospital, 42 Dorsey Street, Montgomery, I want to see you at once. Yours truly, Bill Traylor."

Q. You went to see him?

A. The place was a large old two-story house with a wide hall down the middle, rooms off to each side. I went down the hall and it was the last room on the left, a very big room, like a ward with cots lined up. There must have been a dozen other people in the room. A black woman was there, a nurse.

Q. This was an all-black nursing home?

A. Yes. It was an awful place. Bill could hardly talk, there wasn't any real conversation. I remember kneeling down beside him and he could barely speak. I can't even remember now what was said. That was the last time I saw him. In just a few days, his daughter called to say that he had died. He was already buried when she called me, so I didn't get to go to the funeral.

Q. Did you ever get any sense of what got him working in the first place? Where did that first spark come from?

A. As I see it, because of the restrictions of his age, his rheumatism, and his circumstances in general, he was

FIGURE CHASING A BIRD
Poster paint and pencil on cardboard
12" × 9"

stalemated. In a moment when he could make no move, so to speak, he found a stub of a pencil, a piece of cardboard, and a little stick—items easily come by on Monroe Street. He ruled a line. When he saw the mark, engraved straight and clean into the soft cardboard, it happened. . . . The mark pleased him. He added another mark. Parallel lines. Order. Somewhere in the depths of his sensibilities the energy of the marks struck home. He became awake to the powers of visual language. It must have been exciting to him because he didn't stop drawing.

Q. In speaking of Traylor's beginning to draw, we are reminded of the famous misquote.

A. You must be referring to the 1946 *Colliers* article. A newspaperman came to me and told me that Traylor wouldn't talk to him and asked me to fill him in on his story. He wanted to know how it all came to happen, and I said, "I don't know, it just came to him." He wrote: "Traylor said, 'It jes' come to me.'" Being the only nationally circulated story about Traylor in those times, it is now the one uncovered by researchers and has been quoted many times in the last few years.

Q. How about the rest of the article? Were there other inaccuracies?

A. Yes. For example: in telling the story about my taking Bill to see his exhibition at New South, the *Colliers* story goes this way: "They went and got old Bill off his street corner and bought him a white collar. They led him, looking for all the world like old Black Joe, into the better part of town. Finally, they helped him up two flights of stairs, into the brightest, whitest room he had seen since Christmas mornings back in old master's house. . . ." Elsewhere, the article has Traylor saying, "Whoa mule, stand still—Ise gwina draw ya pitcher." Traylor never looked at anything while drawing it, he waited until it jes' come to him.

Q. It appears, then, that after his New South show in 1940, this article was the nearest thing to recognition Traylor received in his lifetime.

A. Well, his highest recognition came in 1942 when director Alfred Barr and his staff selected sixteen Traylor drawings for the Museum of Modern Art. Even though it happened that the drawings never became part of the Museum Collection, they did receive that approbation.

Q. What happened?

A. On a trip to New York in 1941 I carried a large group of Traylor drawings to show to friends, one of whom directed me to a man on the staff of the Museum of Modern Art. The man was interested in the work and arranged an exhibition of it at the Fieldston School in New York, with which he was also associated. (Bill received a ten-dollar "rental fee" for this.) Later, Alfred Barr and his staff were shown the drawings. Without ever consulting me as to whether or not I wanted to sell the work or, if so, at what prices, I simply received a check with a letter telling me that Mr. Barr and staff had "agreed to pay $2 a piece for the larger drawings and $1 for the smaller ones. We are enclosing a check for $20.50 for those . . . selected by staff members. . . . Sixteen others were selected for the Museum Collection and a check will be sent to you by the Museum. If you have a better arrangement will you let us know and we will be glad to follow it. I hope this meets your approval." Taken aback, I returned the check and demanded immediate return of my drawings.

Q. Did you get them back?

A. I did. Here is the correspondence . . . on Museum of Modern Art stationery.

Q. I wonder if you had gone along with that, if the career, so to speak, of Traylor would have taken a different turn?

A. Yes, it probably would have. From this perspective I guess my handling of the matter was a mistake.

Q. After Traylor died, you found yourself with the bulk of Traylor's work. Do you know about how many pieces he produced?

A. I have said earlier, in answer to that question, from 1,200 to 1,500. I think now the lower figure is probably about right.

Q. You've said that having the work created problems. How did you mean that?

A. Storage was a problem. Everywhere I went, I had boxes of street-dirty cardboard to move with me. Mainly, there was the problem of having this work I thought was beautiful and important and I couldn't figure out a way to get it out into the world.

Q. Of course, after World War II, it was no help to the Traylor cause when abstract expressionism hit the scene with a bang.

A. In the late forties and for years to come, it completely dominated the art climate. Work such as Traylor's was not given the time of day. So I stored it away, keeping out a few drawings for my own enjoyment.

Q. Then a time came when you brought it out again.

A. Twenty-five years later, in the mid-seventies, I got the drawings out to show to Gina, my wife, who had seen only a few of them. She was excited by them and so was I, all over again.

Q. By this time much had changed. Did you feel that there might be more receptivity to Traylor's work?

A. We did, so we set about cataloguing,

cleaning, and otherwise putting the body of work in orderly condition to prepare it for public exposure. We tried in various ways to attract interest in the work, but without success until 1979. In that year, a new gallery on New York's 57th Street presented Traylor's work in a one-man show, then it closed almost immediately. A few sales were made, however, and some favorable reviews were written. In 1982, thirty-six Traylors were included in the Corcoran Museum's *Black Folk Art in America, 1930–1980* exhibition, which toured the country, and Traylor emerged as the critics' "star of the show." In the years that have followed, his work has been widely shown, acclaimed, and collected all over this country and in Japan and Europe.

Q. Going back to the photographs of Traylor drawing, you said you used to sit on this box beside him and watch him work. Did you chat with him during those times?

A. Oh yes. There was a lot of silence, but sometimes he would just start talking, he would tell me a story or we'd have a little discussion about something. I remember one story he told. He said, "The old bullfrog got up one evening and said, 'I've got to leave this pond for a few days. Who's going to sleep with my wife while I'm gone?' And all the little frogs said, 'Meeee . . . meeee . . .' Then the old frog said, 'Who's going to work and take care of my wife while I am gone?' . . . and I ain't heard a sound till yet."

Q. We know that he occasionally made comments about his drawings and you jotted down his remarks on the backs of the drawings after you left him. They would offer a way to hear him. Could you read a few of them to us?

A. On the back of a mule it says, "He hear sompin'. Come up on one at night and he'll sho' see you 'fo you see him." On another drawing of a mule (page 27), "He's sullin'. He won't work. Minute he sees a plow he start swinging back. You can't make him go. Gits that pride from his mama. Everywhere dat mare went, he went, followed her everywhere . . . so when he got big . . . he just like her . . . went everywhere she went . . . did everything she did." On another one, he says, "Old lady fussed at him so much he came out in the yard to read and she come after him. The little girl listened to what she tell him." And about Ross, the undertaker, "When he comes in, he always looks around seein' if dem boxes is empty."

Q. His imagery seemed to just well up from the experiences of his long life. Some seemed to be based on

"HE'S SULLIN'"
Poster paint and pencil on cardboard
$11^{3}/8'' \times 17^{1}/4''$

BLACK MAN LEADING BROWN DOG
Poster paint and pencil on cardboard
14″ × 21¹/₂″

memories of specific people or animals, others were obviously inventions.

A. In the former category many of his animal drawings, particularly horses, mules, and dogs, were of specific animals: the old horse who was "turned out in the pasture to die" and the mule who "won't work." Such as these were quite naturalistically drawn. Nothing else he ever drew was done so realistically. Some of the people he drew were people he knew or had seen, habitués of the Monroe Street sidewalks. Aside from people and animals, it is obvious that his houses, baskets, and abstract forms are inventions. One subject he drew more than once was, he told me, a construction they made by the river when he was young. They would run out on it and dive in the river, come out and take a drink, and return to dive in again. The construction he drew, however, was an abstract invention. His "Blacksmith Shop" was done in terms of an array of the tools of the shop. He did not draw places. Once he had drawn a house with a man seen through a doorway, reading. He said he had been thinking for some time about how to draw a man inside of a house. After he found a way, he used it many times in later drawings. On a fine spring day I went by and he was drawing a man plowing. He said, "I wanted to be plowing so bad today, I draw'd me a man plowing."

Q. What were some of Traylor's styles?

A. In the first weeks, when he used only pencil, we get the lined-up objects, the best example of which is the large version of the "Blacksmith Shop" (page 13). Then came a series of what I called "Exciting Events." A typical example would be one he did several versions of: a big snake and several fleeing figures, children, old people with canes, and dogs all running and screaming. And there were other storytelling pictures such as possum hunts and drinking bouts. Soon after he got his showcard colors, he had his abstract period. His "basket" period came in the summer of 1939, all sorts of forms, usually with a thatch pattern, sometimes with plant or animal forms, made "baskets." The animals—cows, horses, mules, dogs, and cats—came early and recurred periodically all during his time of productivity; so did drawings of men, women, and combinations of the two.

Q. You have said that there was a burst of doing all the animals he knew.

A. Some of them he said he had never seen except on circus posters and billboards. He did a camel from a package of cigarettes. For a short time he drew plant and animal

Monroe Street, 1939

forms in highly abstracted form. One group of drawings I called "Figures and Constructions" because they were characterized by a geometric shape or construction used in combination with figures and/or animals. These came late, probably during the last year of his working. They brought together many of the visual themes he had developed by this time: strong abstract forms, combination plant-animal and abstract forms, people in various "states" ranging from serenity to hysteria, thieves and drunks and devilish kids. They were done with a sure touch and demonstrate his great mastery of his craft. With these came his most complex compositions and they were full of wonderful humor, both illustratively and in a purely visual way.

Q. Humor is in his work from start to finish. And, as you say, at times the fun is anecdotal, other times it lies in the spatial games being played, or in an arm sprouting leaves, or a wonderful body gesture, or a surprising abstract event.

A. You do have to be responsive to the abstract play as well as the realism to enjoy his work fully.

Q. Maybe this explains why galleries known essentially for their interest in modern art are so enthusiastic about his work. They see it as modern.

A. It seems to have already transcended the labels of "black" and "folk," but the label doesn't matter: the work has carved out a place for itself.

DOG HEAVING
Poster paint on cardboard
11″ × 14″

TWO FIGHTING DOGS
Poster paint and pencil on cardboard
14¹/₄″ × 23″

OPPOSITE:
**THREE FIGURES ON RED
AND BLUE HOUSEBOAT**
Poster paint and pencil on cardboard
15″ × 13″

**BLACK ELEPHANT
WITH A BROWN EAR**
Poster paint on cardboard
14³/₄″ × 26″

**FIGURE/CONSTRUCTION,
MAN IN CHAIR**
Poster paint and pencil on cardboard
13¹/₄″ × 7³/₁₆″

**BLUE CONSTRUCTION,
ORANGE FIGURES**
Poster paint and pencil on cardboard
$19^{3}/_{4}'' \times 7^{1}/_{4}''$

**MAN AND
LARGE DOG**
Poster paint
and pencil on cardboard
(double-sided, verso:
Man and Woman)
28″ × 22″

MAN/BARS
Compressed charcoal
on cardboard
$28^5/_8'' \times 22^1/_2''$

**ABSTRACT CAT
WITH RED EYES**
Poster paint and pencil on cardboard
$10^3/_{16}'' \times 7^1/_{16}''$

OPPOSITE:
TURTLE
Poster paint and pencil on cardboard
$11^3/_4'' \times 7^3/_4''$

44

**FIGURES/CONSTRUCTION,
BLACK, BROWN, RED**
Poster paint and pencil on cardboard
15¹/₄″ × 7¹/₄″

CROUCHED MAN POINTING
Wax crayon on cardboard
$9^{1}/_{4}$" × $7^{7}/_{8}$"

OPPOSITE:

**LARGE FIGURE
WITH GREEN LEGS
WITH OTHER FIGURES
SURROUNDING HIM**
Colored pencil on cardboard
$10^3/_4'' \times 10^1/_4''$

GREEN MAN ON WING FORM
Colored pencil on cardboard
$11^1/_2'' \times 7^3/_4''$

OPPOSITE:

BLUE CAT
Poster paint and pencil on cardboard
15″ × 14″

MAN WITH YOKE
Poster paint and pencil on cardboard
14¼″ × 13½″

GREAT BLACK BULL
Poster paint and pencil on cardboard
12″ × 15″

TWO MEN
Poster paint and pencil on paper
22″ × 14″

54

MAN SPROUTING LEAVES
Compressed charcoal and colored pencil
on cardboard
$11^{3}/_{4}'' \times 7^{3}/_{4}''$

MAN WITH UMBRELLA
Compressed charcoal on cardboard
$10^3/_4'' \times 6^3/_4''$

56

BROWN FIGURES CHASING BIRD UP A CONSTRUCTION
Poster paint and pencil on cardboard
$14^{3}/_{4}'' \times 14''$

OPPOSITE:

BLACK AND RED DOGFIGHT
Poster paint and pencil on cardboard
$27^{1}/_{2}'' \times 22''$

**BROWN DOG
WITH NURSING PUPS**
Poster paint and pencil on cardboard
$7^{1}/_{4}'' \times 13^{1}/_{4}''$

**HOUSE WITH FIGURES
AND ANIMALS**
Colored pencil and pencil
on cardboard
22″ × 13¹/₂″

MAN AND BIRD ON HOUSE
Poster paint and pencil on cardboard
16″ × 14″

62

**BLUE CONSTRUCTION
WITH TWO FIGURES AND DOG**
Poster paint and pencil on cardboard
13¹/₄″ × 7¹/₄″

MAN WITH FINGER RAISED
Poster paint and pencil on cardboard
$12^3/_4'' \times 8''$

SNAKE
Poster paint and pencil on cardboard
$11^{3}/_{4}'' \times 10''$

OPPOSITE:

**BLACK BASKET FORM,
SNAKE, BIRD, AND MAN**
Colored pencil and pencil on cardboard
$11^{1}/_{4}'' \times 10''$

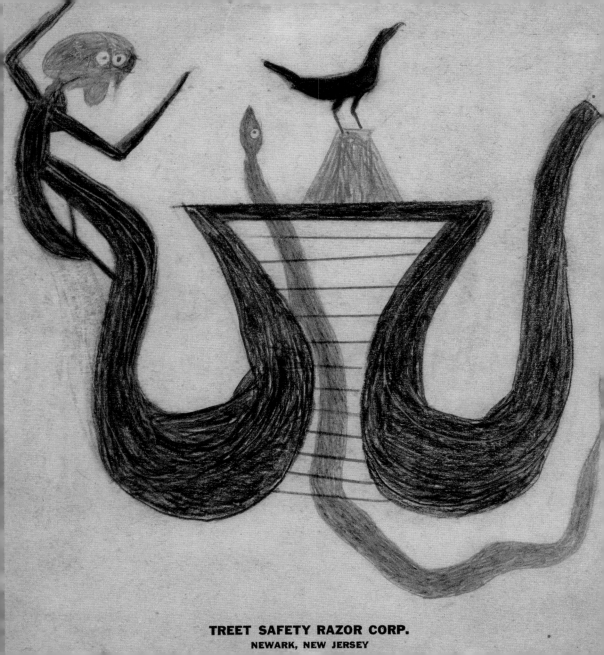

OPPOSITE:

GRAY DOG
Poster paint and pencil
on cardboard
27″ × 28¹/₄″

NRA-WPA
Poster paint and pencil
on cardboard
12¹/₂″ × 8¹/₈″

GREEN AND BROWN HOUSE WITH FIGURES AND DOG

Poster paint and pencil on cardboard

$13^{3}/_{8}'' \times 14^{1}/_{2}''$

**MAN WITH FLIRTATIOUS
WOMAN**
Pencil and colored pencil on cardboard,
with metal hanger
Signed
25¹/₂″ × 13″

OPPOSITE:

**FIGURE/CONSTRUCTION,
MAN STEALING LIQUOR**
Poster paint and pencil on cardboard
12″ × 11″

**OUTLINE OF HOUSE
WITH FIGURES**
Poster paint and pencil on cardboard
14⅛″ × 21¾″

**BLUE CONSTRUCTION
WITH MAN PULLING UP FOOT**
Poster paint and colored pencil on cardboard
15$^{1}/_{4}$″ × 8″

OPPOSITE:

FEMALE DRINKER
Poster paint and pencil on cardboard
11$^{1}/_{2}$″ × 8$^{3}/_{8}$″

SPOTTED CAT, BLACK AND WHITE
Poster paint and pencil on cardboard
9¹/₂″ × 14″

**ONE-ARMED MAN
REACHING FOR BOTTLE**
Pencil, colored pencil,
and poster paint on cardboard
$12^{1}/_{4}'' \times 8^{1}/_{4}''$

76 BROWN HOUSE WITH FIGURES AND BIRDS
Pencil, colored pencil, and poster paint on cardboard
$22^{1}/_{2}'' \times 17^{3}/_{4}''$

**BROWN LAMP
WITH FIGURES**
Poster paint and pencil
on cardboard
13³/₈″ × 7³/₈″

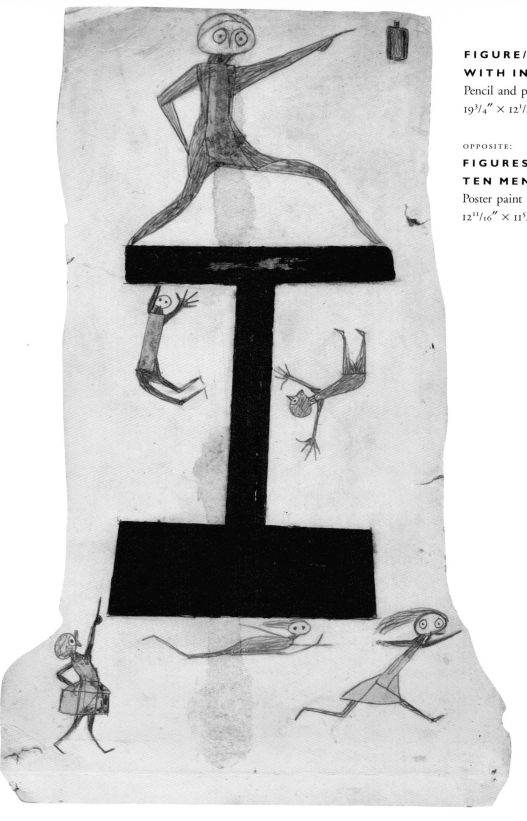

**FIGURE/CONSTRUCTION
WITH INVERTED H**
Pencil and poster paint on cardboard
$19^3/_4'' \times 12^1/_4''$

OPPOSITE:

**FIGURES/CONSTRUCTION,
TEN MEN AND A DOG**
Poster paint and pencil on cardboard
$12^{11}/_{16}'' \times 11^5/_8''$

**BLUE HORSE,
STARTLED**
Poster paint and pencil
on cardboard
$14^{1}/_{4}'' \times 11^{1}/_{4}''$

RADIO
Pencil and poster paint
on cardboard
32¹/₂″ × 42¹/₂″

OPPOSITE:

MULE WITH RED BORDER
Poster paint on cardboard
18^1/$_2$″ × 20^1/$_2$″

SELF-PORTRAIT WITH PIPE
Pencil and colored pencil on cardboard
7^7/$_8$″ × 11^1/$_2$″

**"CEDAR TREES,
LIKE THEY HAVE
SIDE OF DOORS"**
Compressed charcoal on cardboard
21⁷/₈″ × 13⁷/₈″

**FIGURE/CONSTRUCTION
WITH BLUE BORDER**
Poster paint and pencil on cardboard
15^{1}/$_{2}$″ × 8″

86

**EXCITING EVENT,
WOMEN WITH CHILDREN,
TWO MEN WITH JUG**
Pencil on cardboard
21³/₄″ × 14″

OPPOSITE:

**DOG ON RED
BACKGROUND**
Pencil and poster paint on paper
22″ × 28″

OPPOSITE:

**PREACHER AND
CONGREGATION**
Pencil and colored pencil on paper
15¹/₄″ × 13¹/₄″

**ONE-LEGGED MAN
WITH AIRPLANE**
Colored pencil and poster paint
on cardboard
15¹/₂″ × 9³/₈″

**BLUE CONSTRUCTION,
FIGURES AND BOTTLES**
Poster paint and pencil on cardboard
10³/₄″ × 15″

**HOUSE WITH FIGURES
AND DOG**
Poster paint and pencil on cardboard
22″ × 14″

OPPOSITE:

BLACK JESUS

Poster paint and pencil on cardboard

13³/₄″ × 10″

BLACK GEOMETRIC FORM

Poster paint and pencil on cardboard

13″ × 15″

**FIGURES AND
CONSTRUCTION
WITH CAT**
Poster paint on cardboard
13⁷/₈″ × 9″

MAN, WOMAN
Poster paint and pencil on cardboard
$14^{1}/8'' \times 21^{5}/8''$

**MAN IN BROWN AND BLUE
HOUSE WITH FIGURES**
Poster paint and pencil on cardboard
13⁷/₈″ × 21⁷/₈″

RUNNING RABBIT
Poster paint and pencil on cardboard
9³/₄″ × 8″

RED TURKEY
Poster paint and pencil
on cardboard
$9^{3}/_{4}'' \times 7^{5}/_{8}''$

OPPOSITE:

**MAN ON WHITE,
WOMAN ON RED**

Poster paint and pencil on paper
19″ × 24″

WOMAN WITH BIRD

Poster paint and pencil on cardboard
13³/8″ × 7⁵/₁₆″

RED MAN
Poster paint and pencil on cardboard
12″ × 7³/₄″

BIG MAN, SMALL MAN
Pencil and compressed charcoal
on cardboard
13″ × 9¹/₄″

**BLUE CONSTRUCTION,
FIGURES AND DOG**
Poster paint and pencil on cardboard
13$\frac{1}{2}$″ × 7$\frac{1}{4}$″

**BASKET,
MAN AND OWL**
Pencil and colored pencil
on cardboard
14″ × 9″

BLUE MAN READING
Poster paint on cardboard
$11^{1}/_{2}'' \times 7^{3}/_{4}''$

Colored pencil on cardboard
13³/₄″ × 7″

**CONSTRUCTION
WITH LAMPS**
Poster paint on cardboard
$10^3/_4'' \times 7^1/_2''$

ONE-ARMED MAN SEATED
Colored pencil on cardboard
9¹/₄″ × 9¹/₄″

OPPOSITE:

MOTHER WITH CHILD
Pencil and colored pencil
on cardboard
15¹/₂″ × 11³/₄″

112

RABBIT, BLACK AND TAN
Poster paint and pencil on cardboard
$9^{1}/_{4}'' \times 9^{1}/_{4}''$

**WOMAN
WITH GREEN BLOUSE
AND UMBRELLA**
Compressed charcoal
on cardboard
13⁷/8″ × 10⁷/8″

OPPOSITE:

**FIGURE/CONSTRUCTION,
MAN WITH AXE**
Poster paint and pencil on cardboard
9¹/₂″ × 7³/₈″

**TWO WOMEN IN ORANGE,
TWO MEN IN BLUE**
Pencil, colored pencil, and poster paint
on cardboard
14³/₄″ × 26¹/₂″

MAN IN BLUE SUIT
Poster paint and pencil on cardboard
23″ × 12″

**FIGURE/CONSTRUCTION,
BIG BLUE MAN**
Poster paint and pencil on cardboard
22³/₁₆″ × 14″

118

FIERCE DOG WITH BLACK AND RED SPOTS
Pencil and poster paint on cardboard
12″ × 15″

**DOG ATTACKING
MAN SMOKING**
Colored pencil on cardboard
$9^{1}/_{2}'' \times 7''$

YELLOW CHICKEN
Poster paint and pencil on cardboard
$13^{7}/_{8}'' \times 8^{1}/_{4}''$

OPPOSITE:

BOXERS IN BLUE
Poster paint and pencil on cardboard
$20^{7}/_{8}'' \times 22''$

RUNAWAY GOAT CART
Poster paint and pencil on cardboard
$14^{1}/8'' \times 22^{1}/4''$

PLANT/ANIMAL FORM WITH MAN AND DOG
Compressed charcoal and colored pencil on cardboard
11³/₄″ × 7³/₄″

OPPOSITE:

**KITCHEN SCENE,
YELLOW HOUSE**

Pencil and colored pencil
on cardboard

22″ × 14″

**YELLOW AND BLUE
HOUSE WITH FIGURES
AND DOG**

Pencil and colored pencil
on cardboard

22″ × 14″

**SELF PORTRAIT
WITH TWO CANES**
Poster paint and pencil
on cardboard
17″ × 11″

**WOMAN, BLUE GLOVES,
BROWN SKIRT**
Poster paint and pencil on cardboard
9″ × 19¹/₂″

FEMALE ON CHAIR
Poster paint and pencil on cardboard
14$^1/_2$″ × 8″

130 **RED CONSTRUCTION WITH FIGURE AND BIRD**
Poster paint and pencil on cardboard
10^1/$_2$″ × 7^3/$_4$″

Poster paint and pencil
on cardboard
15″ × 12⁷/₈″

OPPOSITE:

MEN ON RED
Poster paint and pencil on cardboard
$28^{1}/_{2}'' \times 22^{7}/_{16}''$

MAN WITH MULE PLOWING
Poster paint and pencil on cardboard
$15'' \times 25^{1}/_{2}''$

134 PIGEON

Poster paint on cardboard
16″ × 8″

**BLACK MAN
ON CONSTRUCTION
POINTING**
Poster paint on cardboard
Signed
13³/₄″ × 6⁷/₈″

LARGE PIG

Poster paint and pencil on cardboard
Signed
$17^{1}/_{4}'' \times 22^{1}/_{2}''$

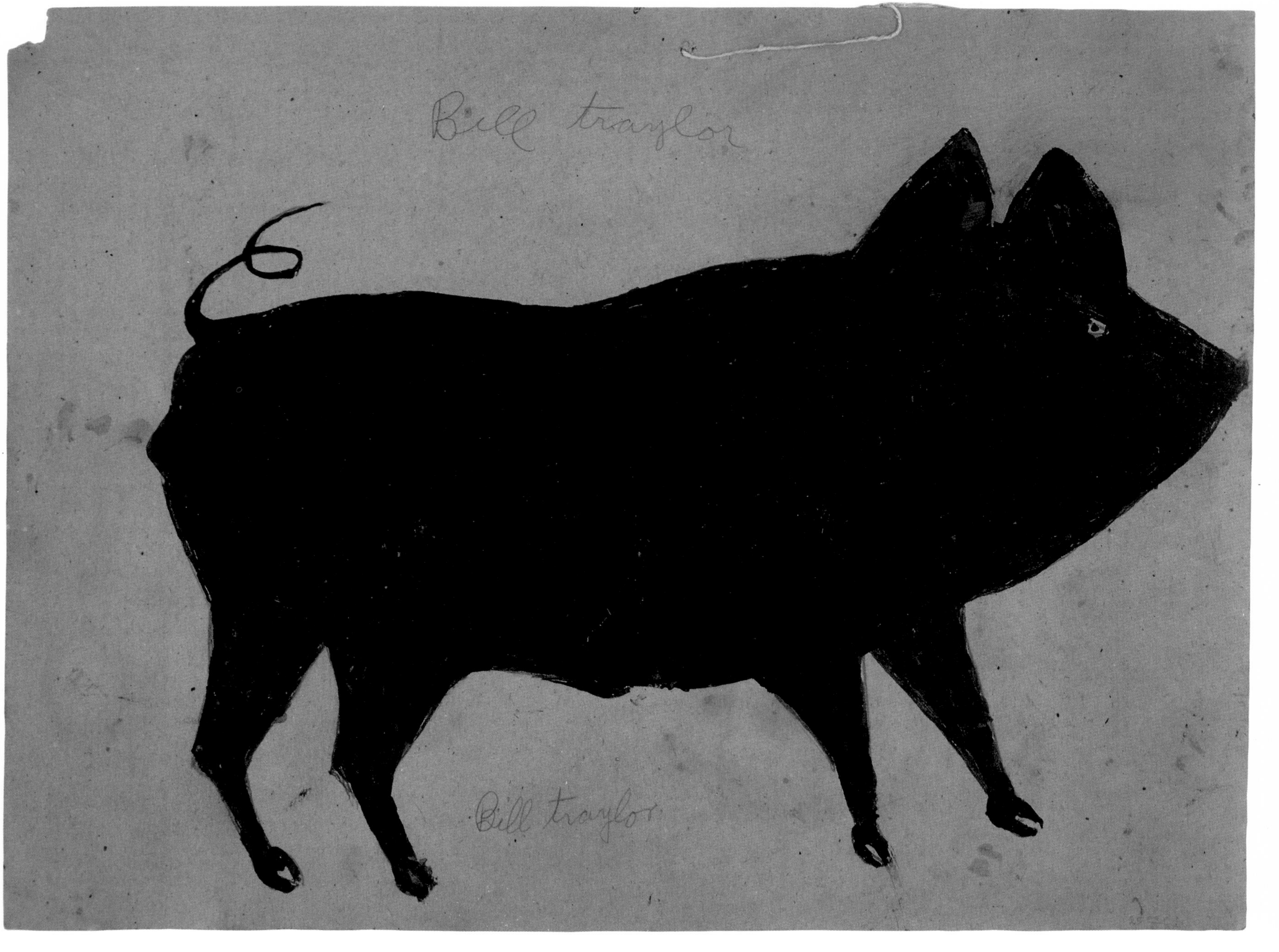

OPPOSITE:

HUNTER ON HORSEBACK
Poster paint and pencil
on cardboard
16½″ × 23″

ABSTRACT TREE WITH FIGURES AND ANIMALS
Pencil and poster paint
on cardboard
22″ × 14″

**MAN IN BLUE HOUSE
WITH ROOSTER**
Poster paint and pencil
on cardboard
15$^3/_4$″ × 11$^3/_4$″

OPPOSITE:

**PREACHING
WITH CIRCLE**
Colored pencil on
cardboard
16″ × 13$^1/_4$″

BLACK MILK COW
Poster paint and pencil on cardboard
11¹/₄″ × 15¹/₂″

TRUNCATED MAN WITH PIPE
Poster paint and pencil on cardboard
9″ × 9¼″

**CHICKEN ATOP
SPECKLED HOUSE**
Poster paint and pencil
on cardboard
22″ × 14″

LEGS CONSTRUCTION WITH FIGURE
Colored pencil on cardboard
$9^1/_8'' \times 9^1/_8''$

OPPOSITE:

FIGURES ON BLUE CONSTRUCTION
Poster paint and pencil
on cardboard
$13^3/_4'' \times 12^3/_4''$

SCARY CREATURE
Compressed charcoal on cardboard
$17^{3}/_{4}'' \times 10^{3}/_{8}''$

OPPOSITE:

THE CHASE
Poster paint and pencil on cardboard
Signed
$15'' \times 14^{1}/_{2}''$

Pencil on cardboard
$10^3/_4'' \times 8''$

**MAN IN BLACK AND BLUE
WITH CIGAR AND SUITCASE**
Poster paint and pencil on cardboard
21¹/₂″ × 16″

**EXCITING EVENT,
HUNTERS AND DRINKERS**
Colored pencil and pencil on cardboard
15″ × 20″

ANIMAL/PLANT FORM, GREEN
Colored pencil and pencil on cardboard
14″ × 11″

154

**EXCITING EVENT,
BLUE MAN, SNAKE**
Colored pencil and pencil
on cardboard
13⁵/₈″ × 22″

OPPOSITE:
**DOGFIGHT
WITH WRITING**
Poster paint and pencil
on cardboard
Signed
21″ × 22″

Bill Taylor

Bill Tralor

Bill Traylor

This Dryling was ~~Known~~ Done By Bill Tralor

Old man . 85 years old

BLACK FISH
Colored pencil on cardboard
Signed
10″ × 8″

LEGS CONSTRUCTION WITH FIVE FIGURES
Colored pencil on cardboard
13¹/₄″ × 7¹/₄″

**MAN/WOMAN, GREEN
BLOUSE, BLUE SHIRT**
Compressed charcoal and colored
pencil on cardboard
19″ × 12″

RED DOG
Poster paint and pencil on cardboard
$31^{1}/_{2}'' \times 17^{1}/_{2}''$

SPREAD LEGGED DRINKER
Poster paint and pencil on cardboard
Signed
9¹/₈″ × 13⁵/₈″

DOUBLE GOAT
Poster paint and pencil on paper
$28^{1}/_{2}'' \times 22^{7}/_{16}''$

MAN RIDING BIRD
Poster paint and pencil on cardboard
17″ × 11″

FIGURE AND DOG AND HOUSE
Poster paint and pencil on paper
14″ × 22″

MAN LEADING DOG
Poster paint and pencil on cardboard
$15^{1}/_{4}'' \times 15^{1}/_{8}''$

OPPOSITE:

**WOMAN IN "O" AND "X"
PATTERN DRESS**
Poster paint and pencil on cardboard
15^{1}/$_{8}$″ × 7^{5}/$_{8}$″

BLACK CAT, WHITE FACE
Poster paint and pencil on cardboard
7^{3}/$_{8}$″ × 13^{3}/$_{8}$″

ANIMATED FIGURE
Compressed charcoal on cardboard
13³/₄″ × 10″

OPPOSITE:

**HOUSE, BLUE FIGURES,
BLUE LAMP**
Poster paint and pencil on cardboard
15″ × 13″

TWO-EYED BLACK CAT WITH COLORED SPOTS
Compressed charcoal, colored pencil, and pencil on cardboard
13^7/$_8$″ × 11″

POSSUM HUNT
Poster paint and pencil
on cardboard
24″ × 13¹/₈″

**BLACK MAN WITH
BIG BLUE BOWL
ON HIS HEAD**
Poster paint and pencil
on cardboard
13³/₈″ × 7³/₈″

176

**FIGURE WITH CONSTRUCTION
ON BACK**
Poster paint and colored pencil on cardboard
12³/₈″ × 8¹/₄″

**RED BIRD ON
CONSTRUCTION**
Poster paint and pencil
on cardboard
$13^3/_4'' \times 10^1/_4''$

CHRONOLOGY

1854 Born a slave on George Traylor's plantation near Benton between Selma and Montgomery, Alabama.

1865 After Civil War, continued to live on Traylor place.

1938 Came to Montgomery at age eighty-four. Worked briefly in shoe factory. Became recipient of welfare and slept in back room of Ross Clayton Funeral Parlor on Monroe Street.

1939 Sat on a sidewalk and began to draw. Seen by Charles Shannon, a young painter, who offered support and preserved his work. Moved his sleeping quarters to a shoe-repair shop just off Monroe Street. Finding shelter under a fruit-stand roof, he spent his days drawing.

1940 His work shown for first time at New South Art Center in Montgomery.

1942 Left Montgomery during World War II to live with his children in Detroit and Washington and other cities in the North. Had leg amputated due to gangrene.

1946 Returned to Montgomery.

1947 Died in a nursing home at ninety-three.

**LADY WITH HANDBAG
AND UMBRELLA**
Poster paint and pencil
on cardboard
21″ × 11″

LIST OF EXHIBITIONS

ONE-MAN EXHIBITIONS

1940 New South Art Center,
Montgomery, Alabama
1941 Fieldston School, New York
1979 R. H. Oosterom Gallery,
New York
1982 Vanderwoude Tananbaum Gallery,
New York
Hammer and Hammer Gallery,
Chicago
Montgomery Museum of Fine
Arts, Montgomery, Alabama
Arkansas Art Center, Little
Rock
Karen Lennox Gallery, Chicago
1983 Mississippi Museum of Art,
Jackson
Gasperi Gallery, New Orleans
Hill Gallery, Birmingham,
Mississippi
1984 Acme Art Gallery, San Francisco
Alexander Gallery, Atlanta
1985–86 Hirschl & Adler Modern,
New York
Luise Ross Gallery, New York
1986 Karsten Greve Gallery, Cologne,
W. Germany

The Mayor Gallery, London,
England
1988 Public Library Cultural Center,
Chicago
Reynolds House & Delta Art
Center, Winston-Salem
North Carolina Museum of Art,
Raleigh
High Museum at Georgia-Pacific,
Atlanta
1988–89 Hirschl & Adler Modern,
New York
Luise Ross Gallery, New York
Acme Art Gallery, Santa Monica
1989 Carl Hammer Gallery, Chicago
J. B. Speed Art Museum,
Louisville
African American Museum,
Hempstead, New York
*Black Folk Art Minnie Evans and
Bill Traylor, Chicago Art Expo
'89,* presented by Hirschl &
Adler Modern, New York,
and Carl Hammer Gallery,
Chicago
Dallas Museum of Art, *Black Art
. . . Ancestral Legacy*
Smithsonian Institution Traveling

Exhibition, Washington, DC,
*African American Artist 1880–
1987 Selections from the Evans-
Tibb's Collection*
Alabama State Council on the
Arts, Montgomery, *The New
South, The New Deal and Beyond*
1991 Gallerie Montenay, Paris, France
Hirschl & Adler Modern,
New York
Carl Hammer Gallery, Chicago
Luise Ross Gallery, New York
Leon Loard Gallery, Montgomery,
Alabama
Janet Fleisher Gallery, Philadelphia

GROUP EXHIBITIONS

1979 R. H. Oosterom Gallery,
New York
1982 Southern Arts Federation, Atlanta,
*Southern Works on Paper, 1900–
1950*
City College of New York, *The
Black Presence in the American
Revolution . . . the Continuing
Revolution*

Janet Fleisher Gallery, Philadelphia, *Twentieth-Century Folk Art*
Corcoran Gallery of Art, Washington, DC, *Black Folk Art in America, 1930–1980*
1983 High Museum of Art, Atlanta, permanent collection
University of Illinois at Chicago, *Artists on the Black Experience*
Hammer and Hammer Gallery, Chicago, *The Isolate Artist in America*
Ricco/Johnson Gallery, New York, *The African-American Image*
1984 University of New Orleans, *Southern Folk Images*
Fleisher Gallery, Philadelphia, *Major Black Folk Artists Chicago Expo '84*
1985 Columbia Museum of Art, Columbia, South Carolina, *Art and Artists of the South. The Robert P. Coggins Collection*
Terra Museum of American Art, Evanston, Illinois, *Two Centuries of American Folk Art*
Greenville County Museum of

Art, Greenville, South Carolina *Art for Greenville, Towards a Southern Collection*
Seton Hall University, South Orange, New Jersey, *A Time to Reap: Late Blooming Folk Artist*
Center Gallery, Bucknell University, Lewisburg, Pennsylvania (traveling), *Since the Harlem Renaissance: 50 Years of Afro-American Art*
Robert M. Hicklin, Jr., Inc., Spartanburg, South Carolina (traveling), *The South on Paper: Line, Color and Light*
1986 Setagaya Art Museum, Tokyo, Japan, *Naivete in Art* (opening expo)
Basel Switzerland Art/Fair '86, presented by Karsten Greve Gallery of Cologne, W. Germany
Robert M. Hicklin, Jr., Inc., Spartanburg, South Carolina, *Black Artists: Five from the South*
1987 Hirschl & Adler Modern, New York, *Intuitive Line*
Galerie St. Etienne, New York, *Folk

Art of This Century*
Carl Hammer Gallery, Chicago, *Drawings by Master Visionaries*
Chicago Art Expo '87, presented by Karsten Greve Gallery, Cologne, W. Germany, and Carl Hammer Gallery, Chicago
Fine Arts Museum of the South, Mobile, *Enisled Visions: The Southern Non Traditional Folk Artist*
1988 *Basel Switzerland Art/Fair '88,* presented by Hirschl & Adler Modern, New York
Chicago Art Expo '88, presented by Carl Hammer Gallery, Chicago
High Museum at Georgia-Pacific Center, Atlanta, *Outside the Mainstream: Folk Art in Our Time*
The Montgomery Museum of Fine Arts, Montgomery, Alabama, *Works by Black Americans*
1989 Lorence-Monk Gallery, New York, *Drawings*
High Museum, Atlanta, *Georgia Collects*

Rooseum, Malmo, Sweden, *What Is Contemporary Art?*
Basel Switzerland Art/Fair '89, presented by Hirschl & Adler Modern, New York
Museum of American Folk Art, New York, *Expressions of a New*

Spirit: Highlights from the Permanent Collection of the Museum of American Folk Art
Lorence-Monk Gallery, New York, *Drawings*
High Museum, Atlanta, *Georgia Collects*

1991 Alabama State Council on the Arts, Montgomery, *Bill Traylor, 1939–1942*
Ricco/Maresca Gallery, New York, *American Self-Taught/Works on Paper*

BROWN SPOTTED COW

Poster paint and pencil on cardboard
8″ × 15³/8″

BIBLIOGRAPHY

1946 Rankin, Allen. "He Lost 10,000 Years," *Colliers,* June 22, 1946

1980 Larson, Kay. *The Village Voice,* Jan. 7, 1980

Coker, Gylbert. "Bill Traylor at R. H. Oosterom," *Art in America,* March 1980

Wallis, Brian. "Bill Traylor," *Arts Magazine,* May 1980

1982 Russell, John. "Black Folk Art in America," *The New York Times,* Feb. 14, 1982

Kurtz, Bruce. "Black Folk Art in America, 1930–1980," *Artforum,* March 1982

"Black Folk Art in America," *Art News,* May 1982

Sloane, Harry Herbert. "Black Magic," *GQ,* May 1982

Livingston, Jane. "Black Folk Art in America, 1930–1980," *American Craft,* June–July 1982

Raynor, Vivien. "Art: Show in Brooklyn Mines Black Folk Vein," *The New York Times,* July 2, 1982

Larson, Kay. "Varieties of Black Identity," *New York Magazine,* August 1982

Raynor, Vivien. "A Gentle Naif from Alabama," *The New York Times,* Sept. 26, 1982

Art News, December 1982

1983 Finore, Diane. "Art by Bill Traylor," *The Clarion,* magazine of the Museum of American Folk Art, Spring–Summer 1983

1984 Johnson, Jay, and William C. Ketchum, Jr. "Just Plain Folk," *Horizon,* March 1984

1985 Cameron, Dan. "History and Bill Traylor," *Arts Magazine,* October 1985

Raynor, Vivien. "Art: Traylor Drawings at 2 Galleries," *The New York Times,* Dec. 20, 1985

1986 Yau, John. "Bill Traylor, Hirschl & Adler Modern," *Art Forum,* March 1986

1988 Shannon, Charles. "Bill Traylor's Triumph," *Art and Antiques,* March 1986, reprinted in *Montgomery,* Mar. 31, 1988

Yau, John. "Les Dessins de Bill Traylor," *Galleries International Edition,* December 1988

Kimmelman, Michael. "Bill Traylor," *The New York Times,* Dec. 1988

1989 DuBois, Peter C. "Who Needs Picasso?: Some Alternatives to 36 Million Dollar Paintings," *Barron's,* Jan. 2, 1989

Hayt-Atkins, Elizabeth. "Bill Traylor," *Art News,* March 1989

Holt, Steven, and Michael McDonough. "Why We Love Folk Art," *Metropolitan Home,* April 1989

Harrison, Helen. " 'Primitive' Works Outside the System," *The New York Times,* Aug. 13, 1989

Walker, Maridith. "Bill Traylor Freed Slave and Folk Artist," *Alabama Heritage,* Fall 1989

Nelson, James R. "The New South, The New Deal and Beyond," *The Birmingham News,* Oct. 1, 1989

PHOTOGRAPHIC CREDITS

49. Collection of Joseph H. Wilkinson.
    Photo courtesy of Cheekwood/Fine
    Arts Center, Nashville.
51. Collection of Galerie Karsten Greve,
    Koln.
    Courtesy of Hirschl & Adler
    Modern, New York.
    Photo Zindman/Fremont.
53. Private Collection.
    Courtesy of Hirschl & Adler
    Modern, New York.
    Photo Zindman/Fremont.
54. Collection of Judy Saslow.
    Photo courtesy of Cheekwood
    Museum, Nashville.
55. Marvill Collection.
    Photo Ricco/Maresca Gallery,
    New York.
56. Marvill Collection.
    Photo Ricco/Maresca Gallery,
    New York.
57. Collection of Patrice Pluto.
59. Marvill Collection.
    Photo Ricco/Maresca Gallery,
    New York.
60. Collection of Luise Ross Gallery,
    New York.
    Photo Ricco/Maresca Gallery,

New York.
61. Collection of Timothy and Pamela
    Hill.
    Photo courtesy of Hill Gallery,
    Birmingham, Mississippi.
62. Marvill Collection.
    Photo Ricco/Maresca Gallery,
    New York.
63. Collection of Hirschl & Adler
    Modern, New York.
    Photo Zindman/Fremont.
64. Collection of Charles and
    Eugenia Shannon.
    Courtesy of Hirschl & Adler
    Modern, New York.
65. Collection of Carl Hammer, Carl
    Hammer Gallery, Chicago.
    Photo courtesy of Carl Hammer
    Gallery, Chicago.
66. Collection of Charles and
    Eugenia Shannon.
    Courtesy of Hirschl & Adler
    Modern, New York.
67. Collection of Charles and
    Eugenia Shannon.
    Courtesy of Hirschl & Adler
    Modern, New York.
68. Collection of Siri Von Reis.

Photo Ricco/Maresca Gallery,
New York.
69. Collection of Hirschl & Adler
    Modern, New York.
    Photo Zindman/Fremont.
70. Collection of Judy Saslow.
    Photo courtesy of Carl Hammer
    Gallery, Chicago.
71. Collection of Elyse Kaftan.
    Photo Ricco/Maresca Gallery,
    New York.
72. Collection of Judy Saslow.
    Photo courtesy of Carl Hammer
    Gallery, Chicago.
73. Private Collection.
    Courtesy of Hirschl & Adler
    Modern, New York.
74. Private Collection.
    Courtesy of Hirschl & Adler
    Modern, New York.
75. Collection of Jeffery Wolf and Jeany
    Nisenholz-Wolf.
    Photo Ricco/Maresca Gallery,
    New York.
76. Collection of Hirschl & Adler
    Modern, New York.
    Photo Zindman/Fremont.
77. Private Collection.

Courtesy of Hirschl & Adler
Modern, New York.

78. Private Collection.
Courtesy of Hirschl & Adler
Modern, New York.

79. Collection of Montgomery
Museum of Fine Arts, Montgomery,
Alabama;
Gift of Charles and
Eugenia Shannon.
Photo Scott Photographic Service.

80. Collection of Yves J. Hyat, Paris.
Courtesy of Hirschl & Adler
Modern, New York.
Photo Zindman/Fremont.

81. Courtesy of Hirschl & Adler
Modern, New York.
Photo Zindman/Fremont.

82. Private Collection.
Courtesy of Hirschl & Adler
Modern, New York.

83. Collection of Siri Von Reis.
Photo Ricco/Maresca Gallery,
New York.

84. Collection of Gregory Amenoff and
Victoria Faust.
Photo Ricco/Maresca Gallery,
New York.

85. Collection of the Museum
of American Folk Art,
New York;
Promised Gift of Charles and
Eugenia Shannon.
Photo John Parnell.

86. Collection of Peter Brams.

87. Collection of Benjamin Baldwin.
Photo Ricco/Maresca Gallery,
New York.

88. Collection of Judy Saslow.
Photo courtesy of Cheekwood
Museum, Nashville.

89. Collection of Siri Von Reis.
Photo Ricco/Maresca Gallery,
New York.

90. Collection of Lanford Wilson.
Photo Ricco/Maresca Gallery,
New York.

91. Private Collection.
Courtesy of Leon Loard Gallery,
Montgomery, Alabama.
Photo Ricco/Maresca Gallery,
New York.

92. Collection of Charles and
Eugenia Shannon.
Courtesy of Hirschl & Adler
Modern, New York.

93. Collection of Hirschl & Adler
Modern, New York.
Photo Zindman/Fremont.

95. Collection of Charles and
Eugenia Shannon.
Courtesy of Hirschl & Adler
Modern, New York.

96. Collection of Montgomery
Museum of Fine Arts, Montgomery,
Alabama;
Gift of Charles and
Eugenia Shannon.
Photo Scott Photographic Service.

97. Collection of Richard Oosterom.
Photo Ricco/Maresca Gallery,
New York.

98. Private Collection.
Photo Ricco/Maresca Gallery,
New York.

99. Private Collection.
Courtesy of Hirschl & Adler
Modern, New York.

100. Collection of Hirschl & Adler
Modern, New York.
Photo Zindman/Fremont.

101. Collection of Montgomery Museum
of Fine Arts, Montgomery, Alabama;
Gift of Charles and Eugenia Shannon.

Photo Scott Photographic
Service.

102. Collection of Janet Fleisher Gallery,
Philadelphia.
Photo courtesy of Norinne
Betjemann.

103. Collection of Judy Saslow.
Photo courtesy of Cheekwood
Museum, Nashville.

104. Collection of Hirschl & Adler
Modern, New York.
Photo Zindman/Fremont.

105. Private Collection.
Photo courtesy of Hill Gallery,
Birmingham, Mississippi.

107. Collection of Judy Saslow.
Photo courtesy of Cheekwood
Museum, Nashville.

108. Private Collection.
Courtesy of Hirschl & Adler
Modern, New York.
Photo Zindman/Fremont.

109. Collection of Luise Ross Gallery,
New York.
Photo Ricco/Maresca Gallery,
New York.

110. Collection of Charles and Debra
Glassman.

Photo Ricco/Maresca Gallery,
New York.

111. Collection of Judy Saslow.
Photo courtesy of Cheekwood
Museum, Nashville.

112. Private Collection.
Courtesy of Hirschl & Adler
Modern, New York.

113. Collection of Hirschl & Adler
Modern, New York.
Photo Zindman/Fremont.

114. Private Collection.
Courtesy of Hirschl & Adler
Modern, New York.

115. Collection of Carl Hammer, Carl
Hammer Gallery, Chicago.
Photo courtesy of Carl Hammer
Gallery, Chicago.

116. Private Collection.
Photo courtesy of Hill Gallery,
Birmingham, Mississippi.

117. Collection of High Museum of
Art, Atlanta; Purchased with Funds
from Mrs. L. Hopkins, Edith G.
& Philip A. Rhodes, and The
Members Guild.

118. Collection of Ellen and Les Kreisler,
Richmond.

119. Collection of Siri Von Reis.
Photo Ricco/Maresca Gallery,
New York.

120. Collection of Eugenia Shannon.

121. Collection of Judy Saslow.
Photo courtesy of Cheekwood
Museum, Nashville.

122. Collection of Ricco/Maresca Gallery,
New York.
Photo Ricco/Maresca Gallery,
New York.

123. Collection of Joseph H. Wilkinson.
Photo courtesy of Cheekwood
Fine Arts Center,
Nashville.

124. Collection of Charles and
Eugenia Shannon.
Courtesy of Hirschl & Adler
Modern, New York.

125. Collection of Charles and
Eugenia Shannon.
Courtesy of Hirschl & Adler
Modern, New York.

127. Collection of Charles and
Eugenia Shannon.
Courtesy of Hirschl & Adler
Modern, New York.

128. Marvill Collection.

Photo Ricco/Maresca Gallery,
New York.

129. Collection of Luise Ross Gallery,
New York.
Photo Ricco/Maresca Gallery,
New York.

130. Private Collection.
Courtesy of Hirschl & Adler
Modern, New York.
Photo Zindman/Fremont.

131. Private Collection.
Courtesy of Hirschl & Adler
Modern, New York.

132. Collection of Montgomery Museum
of Fine Arts, Montgomery, Alabama;
Gift of Charles and
Eugenia Shannon.
Photo Scott Photographic Service.

133. Collection of Didi and David
Barrett.
Photo Ricco/Maresca Gallery,
New York.

134. Private Collection.
Courtesy of Hirschl & Adler
Modern, New York.

135. Collection of Patrice Pluto.
Photo Ricco/Maresca Gallery,
New York.

137. Private Collection.
Photo Ricco/Maresca Gallery.

138. Private Collection.
Courtesy of Hirschl & Adler
Modern, New York.
Photo Zindman/Fremont.

139. Private Collection.
Photo courtesy of Hill Gallery,
Birmingham, Mississippi.

140. Private Collection.
Courtesy of Hirschl & Adler
Modern, New York.

141. Collection of Roger R. Ricco.
Photo Ricco/Maresca Gallery,
New York.

143. Collection of Siri Von Reis.
Photo Ricco/Maresca Gallery,
New York.

144. Collection of Robert M. Greenberg.
Photo Ricco/Maresca Gallery,
New York.

145. Private Collection.
Photo courtesy of Hill Gallery,
Birmingham, Mississippi.

146. Collection of High Museum of Art,
Atlanta; Purchased with Funds from
Mrs. L. Hopkins, Edith G. & Philip
A. Rhodes, and The Members Guild.

147. Collection of Charles and
Eugenia Shannon.
Courtesy of Hirschl & Adler
Modern, New York.

148. Collection of the Montgomery
Museum of Fine Arts, Montgomery,
Alabama; Gift of Charles and
Eugenia Shannon.
Photo Scott Photographic Service.

149. Collection of Timothy and Pamela
Hill.
Photo courtesy of Hill Gallery,
Birmingham, Mississippi.

150. Private Collection.
Courtesy of Hirschl & Adler
Modern, New York.
Photo Zindman/Fremont.

151. Collection of Phillip and Frances
Huscher.
Photo courtesy of Carl Hammer
Gallery, Chicago.

152. Private Collection.
Photo Ricco/Maresca Gallery,
New York.

153. Collection of Hirschl & Adler
Modern, New York.
Photo Zindman/Fremont.

154. Collection of Trisha Hammer.

155. Marvill Collection.
Photo Ricco/Maresca Gallery,
New York.

156. Collection of Siri Von Reis.
Photo Ricco/Maresca Gallery,
New York.

157. Collection of Judy Saslow.
Photo courtesy of Carl Hammer
Gallery, Chicago.

159. Private Collection.
Courtesy of Hirschl & Adler
Modern, New York.

160. Collection of Patricia and Mark
McGrath, Chicago.
Photo courtesy of Carl Hammer
Gallery, Chicago.

161. Collection of Trisha Hammer.

163. Collection of Montgomery Museum
of Fine Arts, Montgomery, Alabama;
Gift of Charles and
Eugenia Shannon.
Photo Scott Photographic Service.

164. Collection of Herbert Hemphill.
Photo Ricco/Maresca Gallery,
New York.

165. Collection of Luise Ross Gallery,
New York.
Photo Ricco/Maresca Gallery,
New York.

167. Collection of Petry/Mills.
Photo courtesy of Carl Hammer
Gallery, Chicago.

168. Collection of Siri Von Reis.
Photo Ricco/Maresca Gallery,
New York.

169. Collection of Richard Burns.
Photo Ricco/Maresca Gallery,
New York.

170. Collection of Dr. and Mrs. Meredith
Sirmans.
Photo Ricco/Maresca Gallery,
New York.

171. Collection of Marianne and Sheldon
B. Lubar.
Photo courtesy of Carl Hammer
Gallery, Chicago.

173. Collection of Judy Saslow.
Photo courtesy of Cheekwood
Museum, Nashville.

174. Collection of Judy Saslow.

Photo courtesy of Cheekwood
Museum, Nashville.

175. Collection of High Museum of Art,
Atlanta; Purchased with Funds from
Mrs. L. Hopkins, Edith G. & Philip
A. Rhodes, and The Members Guild.

176. Collection of Judy Saslow.
Photo courtesy of Cheekwood
Museum, Nashville.

177. Collection of Luise Ross Gallery,
New York.
Photo Ricco/Maresca Gallery,
New York.

180. Collection of Joan Lowenthal.
Photo Ricco/Maresca Gallery,
New York.

184. Collection of Charles and
Eugenia Shannon.
Photo Scott Photographic Service.

186. Collection of Charles and
Eugenia Shannon.
Photo Scott Photographic Service.

194. Collection of Luise Ross.
Photo Ricco/Maresca Gallery,
New York.

A NOTE ON THE TYPE

The text of this book was set in Garamond, a
modern rendering of the type first cut by
Claude Garamond (c. 1480–1561). Garamond
was a pupil of Geoffroy Tory and is believed to
have based his letters on the Venetian models,
although he introduced a number of important
differences, and it is to him we owe the letter
which we know as "old style." He gave to his
letters a certain elegance and a feeling of
movement that won for their creator an
immediate reputation and the patronage of
Francis I of France.

Composed by The Sarabande Press, New York
Separated by Reprocolor Llovet, Barcelona
Printed and bound by Kingsport Press, Inc.,
Kingsport, Tennessee

Designed by Peter A. Andersen